# Festivals *of the* World

# THAILAND

Gareth Stevens Publishing
**MILWAUKEE**

Written by
**HARLINAH WHYTE**

Designed by
**LOO CHUAN MING**

Picture research by
**SUSAN JANE MANUEL**

First published in North America in 1998 by
**Gareth Stevens Publishing**
1555 North RiverCenter Drive, Suite 201
Milwaukee, Wisconsin 53212 USA

For a free color catalog describing Gareth
Stevens' list of high-quality books and multimedia
programs, call
1-800-542-2595 (USA)
or 1-800-461-9120 (Canada).
Gareth Stevens Publishing's Fax: (414) 225-0377.
See our catalog, too, on the World Wide Web:
http://gsinc.com

© TIMES EDITIONS PTE LTD 1998
Originated and designed by
Times Books International
an imprint of Times Editions Pte Ltd
Times Centre, 1 New Industrial Road
Singapore 536196
E-mail: te@corp.tpl.com.sg
Printed in Singapore

Library of Congress Cataloging-in-Publication Data:
Whyte, Harlinah.
Thailand / by Harlinah Whyte.
p. cm.—(Festivals of the world)
Includes bibliographical references and index.
Summary: Describes how the culture of Thailand is
reflected in its many festivals, including Songkran,
Loy Krathong, and the Surin Elephant Round-up.
ISBN 0-8368-2009-6 (lib. bdg.)
1. Festivals—Thailand—Juvenile literature. 2.
Thailand—Social life and customs—Juvenile
literature. [1. Festivals—Thailand. 2. Holidays—
Thailand. 3. Thailand—Social life and customs.]
I. Title. II. Series.
GT4878.A2W47 1998
394.269593—dc21                    97-34016

1 2 3 4 5 6 7 8 9 02 01 00 99 98

# CONTENTS

# It's Festival Time . . .

The Thai word for "festival" is ***ngan phi thee*** [gahn pee tee], meaning "work ceremony." Many Thai festivals celebrate the yearly cycle of rice-farming, when everyone comes together to work in the fields. But even when Thais are thinking about work, their love of fun is never far away! Come and ride an elephant into battle, feed some scary ghosts, and get very, very wet! It's ngan phi thee time in Thailand . . .

# WHERE'S THAILAND?

The Kingdom of Thailand is in Southeast Asia. At the heart of the country is the Chao Phraya River **delta**, where Thai farmers grow rice and other crops in the fertile soil. The capital, Bangkok, is in this region.

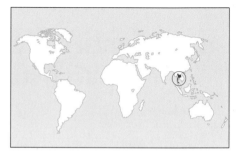

It's hot all year round in Thailand. During the summer months, the **monsoon** brings heavy rains that flood the rivers and help the crops to grow. In the northwest, rain forests cover the mountains and provide a home for tigers, leopards, and wild pigs.

## Who are the Thai?

Thais are famous for their friendly smiles.

All the people of Thailand call themselves Thai, but they come from many different backgrounds. Over the centuries, people from China, Laos, India, Myanmar, Cambodia, and the Malay Peninsula settled in the area. The majority of Thais are descended from people who came from southern China over 1,000 years ago.

Most Thais live in cities or on farms. There are also tribes, such as the Hmong and Akha, who live in the mountains and rain forests. They have their own customs and religions.

4

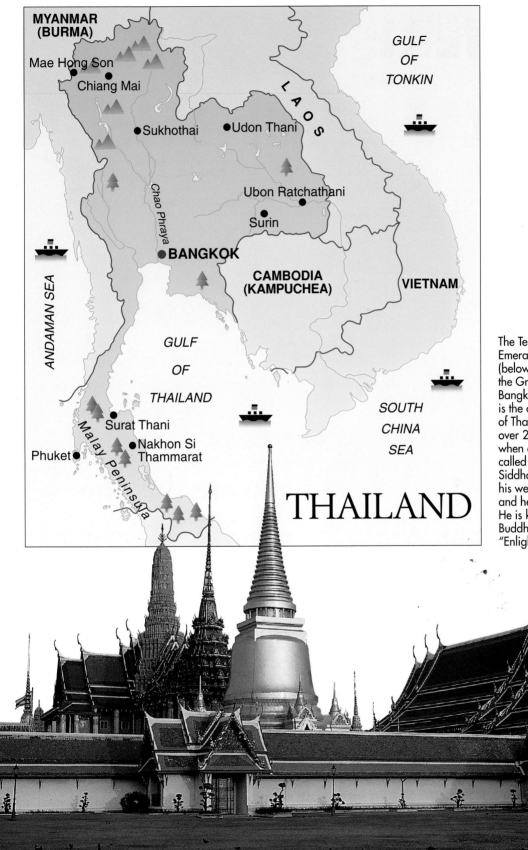

MYANMAR
(BURMA)

Mae Hong Son

Chiang Mai

Sukhothai

LAOS

Udon Thani

GULF
OF
TONKIN

Ubon Ratchathani

Surin

Chao Phraya

BANGKOK

ANDAMAN SEA

CAMBODIA
(KAMPUCHEA)

VIETNAM

GULF

OF

THAILAND

Surat Thani

Nakhon Si
Thammarat

Phuket

Malay Peninsula

SOUTH

CHINA

SEA

THAILAND

The Temple of the
Emerald Buddha
(below) is located at
the Grand Palace in
Bangkok. Buddhism
is the official religion
of Thailand. It began
over 2,500 years ago
when an Indian prince
called Gautama
Siddhartha gave up
his wealth to teach
and help other people.
He is known as
Buddha, which means
"Enlightened One."

# WHEN'S THE NGAN PHI THEE?

*We're from the Akha tribe, and we love to dance! Let's party!*

Thailand's mixed culture has resulted in a mixed calendar of festivals. Some festivals follow the Gregorian calendar (the one we use). Songkran (on page 8) follows the traditional Thai **solar** calendar. Loy Krathong (on page 16) and Ngan Duan Sib (on page 20) follow a **lunar** calendar. And the date of the Royal Plowing Ceremony (on page 14) is decided each year by **Brahman** priests in the royal court.

## SPRING

- ✪ **POY SANG LONG**—Boys in the town of Mae Hong Son dress in colorful costumes and are carried to temples to become monks.
- ✪ **SONGKRAN**
- ✪ **ROYAL PLOWING CEREMONY**
- ✪ **ROCKET FESTIVAL**—Villagers in north-eastern Thailand build huge firecrackers made of bamboo and homemade gunpowder. They fire the rockets into the sky to bring rain.
- ✪ **VISAKHA PUJA**—Buddhists celebrate the anniversary of Buddha's birth, enlightenment, and death with candlelight parades around the temples.

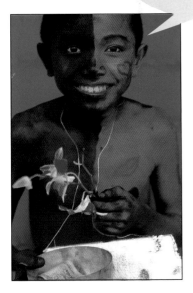

*Ghosts are coming out to play at Ngan Duan Sib! Come and get scared on page 20!*

## SUMMER

✪ **PHI TA KHON**—People dress as ghosts and carry a statue of Buddha through the streets while monks tell an ancient Buddhist story.

✪ **CANDLE FESTIVAL**—Monks in Ubon make large, carved candles and hold a parade to mark the beginning of three months of meditation.

✪ **ASALAHA PUJA**—This Buddhist festival commemorates Buddha's first sermon.

✪ **THE QUEEN'S BIRTHDAY**—Buildings are decorated with lights to celebrate Queen Sirikit's birthday. This is also Mother's Day in Thailand.

*Come for a ride at the Chiang Mai Flower Festival.*

## AUTUMN

✪ **NGAN DUAN SIB**

✪ **VEGETARIAN FESTIVAL**— Chinese Buddhists in Phuket show their devotion by piercing their cheeks with spears and walking on hot coals.

✪ **LOY KRATHONG**

✪ **SURIN ELEPHANT ROUND-UP**

## WINTER

✪ **THE KING'S BIRTHDAY**

✪ **CHIANG MAI FLOWER FESTIVAL**—The flowers of northern Thailand are honored with parades, flower displays, and beauty contests.

# SONGKRAN

T hais love festivals so much, they celebrate New Year twice! The first New Year is on January 1st, just like in most other countries. A few months later, on April 13th, they celebrate Songkran—Thai New Year by the traditional Thai calendar. It's the biggest festival in Thailand—a time for prayers, fireworks, dancing, and lots of water!

## A fresh start to the year

The day before Songkran, everyone gives their house a thorough spring-cleaning. Worn-out clothing and garbage are burned so they won't carry bad luck into the new year.

The Songkran celebrations last for three days. During this time, water is used to purify people and objects. Statues of Buddha are bathed with water. Young people show their respect for older people by pouring perfumed water into the hands of elders. But the biggest displays of water can be found in the street—if you don't mind getting wet!

The Songkran water-splashing ritual used to be very quiet and dignified, but it has turned into a huge water fight. These children have come prepared for some serious Songkran fun.

# Watch out for the water serpents!

An old Thai story tells of serpents called ***nagas*** [NAH-gahs]. The nagas brought rain by spouting water from the sea. The more they spouted, the more rain fell on the land. You probably won't see any nagas today, but at Songkran, children take the place of nagas and shower everyone with water!

Thailand is a noisy, happy, and WET place during Songkran. All over the country, young people toss water at each other and at people on the street. Sometimes they even throw flour. No one is safe! But since Songkran is held in the hottest month of the year, everyone enjoys the chance to have fun and cool off.

*Above: It's impossible to stay dry during Songkran!*

Bathing a statue of Buddha.

Peddlers sell caged birds at temples and on the street. Pay your money, open the basket, and the birds fly away!

# Merit-making

Thais believe that when they die, their spirit leaves their body and enters the body of a new baby. If they are good during their life, their spirit will bring good fortune to their new life. But if they are bad, their new life will be difficult. Thais try to earn spiritual rewards for their future lives by doing good things. This is called **merit-making**.

Songkran is an important time for merit-making. One way to make merit is to be kind to other living creatures. At festivals, people make merit by releasing caged birds and live fish. Giving food to monks, bathing Buddha statues, and making offerings at temples are other ways of making merit.

During Songkran, people bring sand to the temples and build small, sacred sand-domes. Each one is topped with a prayer flag. This boy's flag shows the 12 animals of the Chinese calendar. Each animal represents a different year in a 12-year cycle. The first 11 animals are the same in China and Thailand—rat, ox, tiger, rabbit, dragon, snake, horse, goat, monkey, rooster, and dog. But the last animal is different—the Chinese have a boar, but the Thai have an elephant!

A Songkran parade crosses a river.

# The big parade

In Chiang Mai, huge crowds gather to enjoy the spectacular Songkran parades, with dancers, floats, and bands. A Songkran Queen is chosen to lead the celebrations. The noisy, colorful parade moves through the city as spectators throw water at everyone.

# Angel calendars

Older Thais use a traditional Songkran calendar that has seven angels representing different years. The angels are the seven daughters of a god called Thao Kabillaprom. Each angel has her own day of the week, gemstone, flower, food, and animal to ride on. A different angel represents each year, depending on which day of the week Songkran falls. So if Songkran falls on a Monday, it will be the year of the Monday angel.

### Think about this

The custom of releasing fish into the rivers goes back to an old farming tradition. When the rice fields dried up after the rainy season, baby fish were trapped in small pools of water. The farmers caught the fish and kept them at home until Songkran, when they released them into the river. By doing this, the farmers made merit and preserved the supply of fish (an important food) at the same time.

# ROYAL FESTIVALS

Whether it's an ancient farming ceremony, a majestic river parade, or a fireworks display for the king's birthday, royal festivals attract huge crowds. The biggest celebrations are held in Bangkok. Come and see!

King Bhumibol making an offering at a Buddhist altar.

## Honoring the king and queen

No matter where you go in Thailand, you'll see pictures of King Bhumibol and Queen Sirikit. Thais love their king and queen, and they honor them by placing their pictures in homes and shops and on billboards.

King Bhumibol leads a very busy life. He travels all over the country to help his people, and he continues to perform the ancient ceremonies of the kingdom.

Holding portraits of King Bhumibol and Queen Sirikit at the king's birthday celebrations.

# The King's Birthday

The King's Birthday parade.

December 5th is King Bhumibol's birthday, a day of great celebration in Thailand. Pictures of the king are placed all around town. The Grand Palace and other buildings are decorated with colored lights. In a field near the Grand Palace, thousands of people enjoy stage shows, fireworks, and movies on giant screens. The official celebration in Bangkok includes a parade that is shown on television all over the country.

# The Royal Barge Procession

On very special occasions, the king and over 1,000 officers, oarsmen, and attendants float down the Chao Phraya River in 53 golden barges. Each wooden barge is ornately carved and decorated with gold leaf. In recent years, processions have been held to celebrate the king's 60th birthday (in 1987) and 50th year of rule (in 1996).

The royal barge on the left is called Subanahongsa. It is shaped like the mythical animal ridden by the Hindu god Brahma. The barge on the right is Anantanagaraj, shaped like a seven-headed naga. These are two of the highest-ranking royal barges.

# The Royal Plowing Ceremony

In May, King Bhumibol oversees the ancient Plowing Ceremony to mark the beginning of the rice-planting season. This ceremony began in India, but it has been practiced in Thailand for hundreds of years. The ceremony is very important to Thai farmers, because it predicts how much rain will fall and how well the crops will grow. Thousands of farmers come to the Grand Palace to watch.

While the bulls plow the field, the king watches the ceremony from his royal pavilion.

# Predicting the weather

The Phya Raek Nah (Lord of the Festival) leads the ceremony. When he arrives at the field, he chooses between three *panungs* [pah-NOONGS]. If he chooses the shortest panung, there will be lots of rain. If he chooses the medium panung, there will be moderate rain. But if he chooses the longest panung, there will be little rain, and the farmers know it will be a hard year.

The Phya Raek Nah scatters rice seed on the field.

**Think about this**

The Phya Raek Nah predicts the amount of rain, but the bulls predict which crops will grow well. After the plowing, the bulls are offered plates of rice, beans, corn, hay, sesame seed, water, and wine. Whichever the bulls choose to eat or drink will be plentiful during the next year.

# Plowing the field

Since this is no ordinary plowing, the plow and bulls are special, too. The sacred plow is painted red and gold, and the two bulls are decorated with gold cloth and tassels. As they plow three furrows in the soil, they are accompanied by a procession of drummers, umbrella-bearers, and Brahmans who chant and blow conch shells. Four women carry the rice seed onto the field in gold and silver baskets.

After the plowing, the Phya Raek Nah scatters rice seed on the field. Then the barriers are lowered and hundreds of people rush onto the field to collect the rice. Even if a farmer finds only one grain, he will take it home and mix it with his own rice to ensure a good crop in the coming year.

Carrying the rice seed in silver baskets.

# LOY KRATHONG

On a full-moon night in November, every river in Thailand is covered with hundreds of glowing, bobbing lights. Look closer, and you'll see that the light is coming from floating **krathongs** [gra-tongs]— little cups shaped like **lotus** flowers, each with a candle and incense sticks inside. This beautiful festival is called Loy Krathong, meaning "floating krathongs." Thais believe that floating a krathong will bring them good luck.

## Listen to a story . . .

Seven hundred years ago, Sukhothai was the capital of Thailand. The king of Thailand lived there in his palace. When the rice fields were flooded and the rice had been sown, the farmers of Sukhothai held a festival of floating lanterns.

At that time, a beautiful and skilled woman named Nang Nophamat lived in the king's palace. One year, Nang Nophamat made some special lanterns for the festival. They were made of banana leaves and shaped like lotus flowers. The king was so impressed with her lotus-shaped krathongs, he announced that krathongs would be floated on the river every year from then on.

A young dancer at a Loy Krathong parade.

# Giving thanks for water

Water is very precious in Thailand. The main foods are rice and fish—two things that need lots of water! Rivers and **klongs** [klongs] are an important means of transportation. And, of course, everyone needs water for drinking and washing.

Loy Krathong is held at the end of the monsoon season, when the rivers and klongs are full to overflowing. By placing a krathong on the water, people make an offering to thank the goddess Mae Khongkha (Mother Water). Some people say that Loy Krathong is also a way of saying sorry to Mae Khongkha for having used and polluted the water during the year.

Some people make a wish when they place their krathongs on the water. If the candle keeps burning until the krathongs are out of sight, their wish will come true!

Krathongs come in all shapes and sizes. These intricate krathongs are made in the traditional way, using banana leaves. Some krathongs are small and simple, while others are huge and very fancy.

Children jump into the water to retrieve the krathongs. Maybe this boy will find a coin inside!

# The Loy Krathong song

*On twelfth-month full moon, water overflows the klongs.*
*All of us, men and women, have fun on Loy Krathong!*
*Loy, Loy Krathong, Loy, Loy Krathong.*
*When we have floated our krathongs,*
*We ask the girls to dance ramwong.*
*Ramwong on Loy Krathong Day,*
*Ramwong on Loy Krathong Day!*
*Good deeds will bring us happiness,*
*Good deeds will bring us happiness!*

Schoolgirls light their lanterns for an evening parade.

# Fireworks and races

There's lots happening at Loy Krathong—parades, dancing, beauty contests, boat races, fireworks, and lantern displays. The biggest celebrations happen at Sukhothai. During the evening, a ceremony takes place at the ruins of the old city to remember Nang Nophamat and her first krathongs. The stone pillars and statues are beautifully lit, and hundreds of krathongs are set afloat.

*Opposite:* These dancers are performing in the Loy Krathong parade at Sukhothai.

18

# NGAN DUAN SIB

On a single day in September or October, thousands of ghosts pay a visit to Earth. In the southern town of Nakhon Si Thammarat, people hold a festival to feed the ghosts and send them on their way. It's called Ngan Duan Sib, or Tenth Lunar Month Festival. Watch out—the ghosts are in town!

## Do you believe in ghosts?

Thais believe in all sorts of ghosts and spirits. Some are scary, while others are helpful, playful, or mischievous. *Phii Pret* [pee pret] are ghosts that are released from hell once a year for a brief vacation on Earth. They look frightening, but they're mostly harmless. As punishment for their sins, they have tiny mouths, so they are always hungry. When they come to Nakhon Si Thammarat, people offer them food and gifts to keep them from causing trouble.

All dressed up for the parade.

# A delicious parade

The highlight of Ngan Duan Sib is the special food made for the ghosts. Floats made entirely of food are paraded through town. The floats are decorated with five traditional sweets made in the shape of clothing, jewelry, coins, children's games, and boats (the boats are to help the ghosts sail back across the river of hell). Since the ghosts have such small mouths, there are plenty of thin foods such as *la* [lah], a fine toffee made of rice flour, brown palm sugar, and egg yolks. Offerings made of la are paraded through the streets to the temple, where they are placed on tables in front of the temple. After about five minutes—once the ghosts have finished eating—children are allowed to rush in and help themselves to the sweet la.

A ghost with glowing eyes rides aboard this edible float.

During Ngan Duan Sib, children dress up as ghosts and ask for money. Does this sound like any festival you know?

Taking the sweet, sticky offerings to the temple.

# Dressing up as ghosts

While the parade moves toward the temple, men and children dress up as ghosts and roam the streets, scaring people and asking for money. They wear black body paint and ghostly masks. When the parade reaches the temple, the ghosts are not allowed to come inside.

## Think about this

Many cultures have festivals that welcome ghosts back to Earth for one day each year. Not everyone believes in ghosts, but they enjoy the festivals just the same.

*Right*: Would you give money to this ghost?

*Opposite:* Young participants in the Ngan Duan Sib parade.

23

# SURIN ELEPHANT ROUND-UP

**C**an you imagine a long parade of elephants, colorful dancers, and drummers? Elephants dressed in battle gear going to war? Elephants playing soccer? At the Surin Elephant Round-up in November, you don't have to imagine it—you can see it!

Elephants appear in ancient Thai manuscripts.

## Thailand's most important animal

Elephants have been trained in Thailand for at least 1,000 years. They pull logs in the timber forests and carry heavy burdens. In the old days, kings and generals rode into battle mounted on elephants. The fighting elephants used their long, pointed tusks to attack the enemy. Elephants appear everywhere in Thai art—on statues, paintings, clothes, and silverware, and in literature. White elephants are most highly prized. Anyone who finds a white elephant must give it to the king. The white elephant is bathed, decorated with flowers, fed fruits and sweets, and treated with great respect for the rest of its life.

A **mahout** rides an elephant in the parade at Surin.

# The Elephant Round-up

A colorful parade of elephants and dancers.

The Surin Elephant Round-up is a display of the elephant's intelligence, strength, and obedience. Over 100 elephants take part. There are demonstrations of elephant training and log-pulling, elephant soccer matches, and a tug-of-war between a single elephant and 200 Thai soldiers!

To celebrate the elephant's special place in Thai culture, there are colorful parades of elephants, dancers, and musicians in traditional costumes. The highlight of the day is the parade of elephants and people in battle dress. The costumes are copied exactly from an ancient book on war strategy.

Although they are huge, elephants are surprisingly fast and agile. This elephant is taking part in a soccer match!

# THINGS FOR YOU TO DO

Here's a great Thai game for you to try. Wing Kala is a race, so you'll need a friend or two to join in. In Thailand, Wing Kala is played with coconut shells, but you can use small baskets instead.

The baskets should be firm and strong enough to stand on.

## Here's what you'll need

To play Wing Kala, each person will need two baskets and a piece of string or thin rope about 4 feet (1.2 m) long. Pass one end of the string through a hole in the bottom of a basket. Tie a knot on the inside of the basket.

Take the other end of the string, pass it through the bottom of the other basket, and tie a knot. Make sure that each end of the string is tied securely. Now you're ready to play!

The finished product! The rope is tied securely with a big knot so the basket won't slip off.

Playing Wing Kala
with coconut shells.

# Play Wing Kala

Mark the starting line and the finishing line. Stand
at the starting line with one foot on each basket,
with the string between your first and second
toes. Hold the top of the string in your hands.
When the starter says "Go!," race toward the
finish line. Try not to lose your balance!

## Things to look for in your library

*Arts and Crafts of Thailand.* William Warren and Luca Invernizzi Tettoni (Chronicle Books, 1996).
*Breath of the Dragon.* Gaile Giles and June Otani (Clarion Books, 1997).
*Cooking the Thai Way (Easy Menu Ethnic Cookbooks).* Supenn Harrison and Judy Monroe
   (Lerner Publications, 1986).
*Som See and the Magic Elephant.* Jamie Oliviero and Jo'Anne Kelly (Hyperion, 1995).
*Thailand (New True Books).* Karen Jacobsen (Children's Press, 1990).
*Thailand.* (Video Visits Series).
*Thailand (Where We Live).* Donna Bailey (Steck-Vaughn, 1992).
*Thailand: The Sleeping Angel.* (Thai classical music CD).

# MAKE A KRATHONG

You don't need to have banana leaves to make your own krathong! These paper krathongs are easy to make. Experiment with different colors and designs. Then, on a moonlit night, float your krathong and enjoy a magical Loy Krathong festival with your friends.

## You will need:
1. Thin cardboard
2. A pencil
3. Scissors
4. Glue
5. A small candle
6. A plastic lid or the base of a plastic cup
7. An Xacto knife
8. Flowers with the stems cut off
9. Incense sticks

**1** Draw a large circle on the cardboard, with a smaller circle inside. Draw petals between the two circles. Repeat these steps on another two pieces of cardboard, so that you have three layers.

**2** Cut out the layers. Fold up the petals and arrange the layers on top of each other. Glue the bases together.

**3** Ask a grown-up to help you cut a small cross in the center of the plastic lid or cup. Push the candle through from the bottom so it stands upright.

**4** Place the lid in the center of the lotus and insert the incense sticks. Arrange the flowers in the lotus so they cover the lid.

Important: Never leave a burning candle or incense unattended.

# MAKE WATERMELON SLUSHES

D uring the hot Songkran weather, there's nothing like an icy watermelon slush to cool you down (in between water fights!). This recipe makes four cooling slushes.

## You will need:
1. 6 ice cubes
2. A large slice of seedless watermelon
3. 1 tablespoon sugar or honey
4. A knife
5. A wooden spoon
6. Measuring spoons
7. A blender or food processor

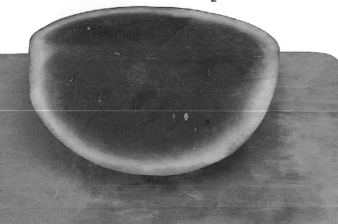

**1** Put the ice cubes in the blender. Ask a grown-up to mix the ice cubes until they are crushed. You may need to stop and use the spoon to help break up the ice.

**2** Ask a grown-up to cut the watermelon into pieces. You'll need about two cups of melon. Add the watermelon to the ice and blend for 1 minute, until the mixture is slushy.

**3** Add the sugar or honey and blend for 10 seconds. Pour the slush into glasses. Now sit back, enjoy your icy slush, and cool off!

# GLOSSARY

| | |
|---|---|
| **Brahman**, 6 | A member of the highest level of Hindu society. Brahmans serve as priests in the royal court of Thailand. |
| **delta**, 4 | The fertile plain where a river meets the sea. |
| *klongs*, 17 | Canals. |
| *krathongs*, 16 | Lotus-shaped cups, traditionally made of banana leaves. |
| *la*, 21 | A sweet toffee offered to ghosts during Ngan Duan Sib. |
| **lotus**, 16 | A type of water lily with a large, beautiful flower. |
| **lunar**, 6 | Based on the phases of the moon. |
| **mahout**, 24 | A person who trains and rides elephants. |
| **merit-making**, 10 | Doing good things in order to gain spiritual rewards. |
| **monsoon**, 4 | A strong seasonal wind that brings heavy rains during summer. |
| *nagas*, 9 | Mythical serpents that bring rain by spouting water from the sea. |
| *ngan phi thee*, 3 | A festival. |
| *panungs*, 14 | Lengths of cloth worn around the hips. |
| *Phii Pret*, 20 | Ghosts that visit Earth during Ngan Duan Sib. |
| **solar**, 6 | Based on the movements of the Sun. |

# INDEX